THE College Student's Cookbook

or

I'm Sick and Tired of That…
What Else Could I Have…

DAVID BAHR

COOL HAND COMMUNICATIONS, INC.
Boca Raton, Florida

ISBN: 1–56790–072–0

First Printing

COOL HAND COMMUNICATIONS, INC.
1098 N.W. BOCA RATON BOULEVARD, SUITE 1
BOCA RATON, FL 33432

Printed in the United States of America.

Cover illustration and book design by Cheryl Nathan.

Bahr, David
The college student's cookbook, or, I'm sick and tired of that—what else could I have—/David Bahr.
p. cm.
Includes index.
ISBN 1-56790-072-0 : $5.95
1. Cookery for one. I. Title. II. Title: College student's cookbook. III. Title: I'm sick and tired of that--what else could I have—.
TX652.B28 1994
641.5'61--dc20
94-22081
CIP

Contents

❦ = A healthy choice (lower fat or cholesterol) for those of you who care about those things.

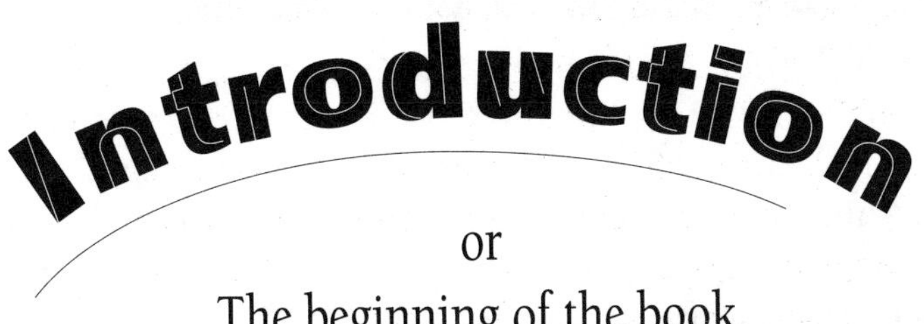

Introduction

or

The beginning of the book.

First of all, a little introduction. This is not a book that will spend most of its time talking about macaroni and cheese, though there will be some discussion about that oldie-but-goodie. It is not a book that will win you cooking awards. You are in college and probably couldn't care less about making a Creole Stuffed Roast (I just looked in a cookbook I have here and opened to that page at random).

What you do care about, if you are like me, is how much time a meal takes to cook, whether or not you can make it with what you have in the fridge, and how many dishes you'll have to wash after you cook it. I have not found any cookbooks which include this very important information. There have actually been days when my dinner selection was determined by what I could cook in one pot, because that was all that was clean.

So this book is for you, even though you probably didn't buy it. The idea is that your relatives will give it to you, because if you were the kind of person who would go out and buy a cookbook, you probably would buy one with a plaid cover that was written by a bunch of chefs or some guy on TV who gets really excited about garlic. And those chefs have no idea how hard it can be to make a meal when you haven't been shopping for two weeks and you can't go tonight because you have an exam, and you're really hungry but there is no way you're going to make spaghetti again, and anyway, you're out of sauce.

This book was written because I realized how many recipes I would never use in the cookbook I got from *Better Homes and Gardens*. And it wasn't because the recipes didn't look good, it was because I just didn't have any basil in the apartment, and didn't have the time to marinate my chicken overnight. I realized other people may have the same problems I had been having for two and a half years of apartment life and two years of dorm life. I've also included some tips on cooking in a slightly more healthy manner, because eating well does make you feel better, and it may help sell the book if your parents are buying it. Then, when your younger siblings go to school, somebody will buy them copies and so on and so forth, and I end up in pretty good shape.

So I wrote this cookbook, and organized it the way I thought would be most useful to a college student. I also included a section on things to buy when you go grocery shopping that make life easier when you cook a meal two weeks later. All of these recipes have been tried at our apartment, and most of my roommates like most of them. Just remember, the food always seems to taste better when you make up part of the recipe, so take a chance every once in a while and add extra of something, or leave out what you don't have, and see how it comes out. I mean, it can't be much worse than some of the pizzas I've eaten around here. Any comments about the recipes by my girlfriend, my roommates, their girlfriends, or other people who have suffered through the earlier stages of some of the recipes were greatly appreciated, so thanks, guys. And if anyone out there wants to let me know how they feel about this, write me or something. If nothing else, mail me some cookies. Good eating, and good luck at school because that's sure a lot more important than making any one of these recipes come out right.

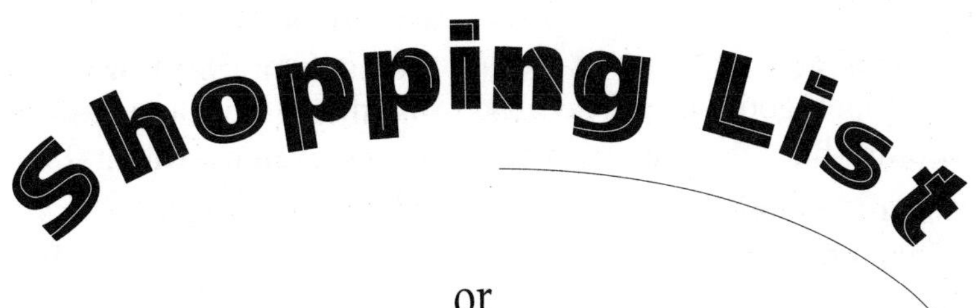

Shopping List

or

Things that get used in a lot of these recipes
so you may want to pick them up, especially if they are on sale.

If you are planing on using this book and you are heading to the grocery store soon, you may want to pick up some of the following stuff. Also listed are the amounts of time they have lasted in my fridge or on my shelf before looking like a biology experiment. These are just the things you may otherwise miss. The standard prepared foods, like macaroni and cheese, soup and frozen orange juice, are not included. Also, fresh fruits are not on this list. Just make sure to buy them in season so they are cheaper. If you plan on using the Meals to Impress Your Date section of this book, check it before Friday afternoon, OK? And if you get sick from something that went bad, don't blame me. If it smells bad, just toss it out. Getting sick isn't worth saving a quarter.

FOODS

Green pepper	a week (in the fridge)
Onions (white or yellow)	about a month or more
Fresh carrots	two or three weeks
Cheese (real, not processed)	two or three weeks

Eggs	two to four weeks
Chicken breasts	freeze them, they'll last for a month; fridge for about 2 days
Ground beef	freeze it, and forever
Frozen pea pods	couple of months
Frozen broccoli	same

BAKING SUPPLIES AND SPICES

(no refrigeration)

Flour	months in a sealed container
Sugar	same
Instant rice	You'll use it before it goes bad.
Baking soda	a year on my last box
Baking powder	till you graduate
Vegetable oil	until it is gone
Pepper	forever
Salt	same
Cream of tartar	same
Cinnamon	same
Cloves	same
Cumin	same
Garlic salt	until you move
Vanilla	even through several moves
Soy sauce	till its gone
Barbecue sauce	a long time
Brown sugar	even longer
Corn starch	ages

Breakfast

or

Everybody gets sick of cereal or bagels once in a while.

Lets face it, sometimes you have time on a weekend, sometimes you just don't want another bagel in the morning, and cereal does run out after a while. So this section will try to add some variation to get your morning (or early afternoon, depending on the night before) off to a good start.

FRENCH TOAST

Eggs	2 is usually fine. For one person, you can get by with one.
Milk	a dash is fine, about a 1/4 cup
Vanilla	a capful, or about 1/2 of a teaspoon
Bread	white or wheat slices, about 4, or as many as it takes (Italian or French bread works really nicely.)
Cinnamon	Optional, but a dash is nice

Butter or no-stick spray stuff in a can

Pots and pans to clean up—1 frying pan, 1 dish that can hold a slice of bread

Get the dish that holds a slice of bread. Break the eggs into the dish, pour in the milk and vanilla, then beat with a fork until they are all blended. Place a bit of butter in the pan (or use the no-stick spray for a slightly lower-fat version) and turn on the heat, low. Put a slice of bread in the egg mixture for about 5 seconds.

Flip it over for another five. If you are going with the funky Italian or French bread and you cut the pieces thick, let it stay a little longer. Put the bread in the pan. Flip it after a couple of minutes. Keep turning it until it's the color you want. Repeat until you run out of bread or mix.

Top your french toast with butter, syrup, cinnamon, or anything else you want.

SCRAMBLED EGGS

Eggs	as many as you want, 3 if you are hungry
Milk	about 1/4 cup, maybe a little less
Butter or no-stick spray stuff	

Pots and pans to clean up—1 frying pan, 1 bowl

Crack the eggs in the bowl. Add milk. Mix with a fork until it is mixed. Put a little butter or spray stuff in the pan, heat it up, and pour the eggs in. Stir them around until they are the consistency you want. Add salt and pepper if you want.

BREAKFAST BURRITO THINGS

Eggs	2 or 3, depending on how hungry you are
Milk	a little bit (less than 1/4 cup)
Green pepper	a very small handful, chopped
Onion	half of a small onion
Cheese	grated, about 1 handful
Tomato	optional, but as much as you want, cut up into bits
Tortillas	2
Salsa	as much as you want

Pots and pans to clean up—1 frying pan

Okay, so this is kinda like the Mc D's things they serve in the morning. But hey, you can copy fast food and make it taste better for a lot less than having to walk down the street and buy it.

Butter the pan, or do something so the food won't stick (spray that no-stick spray on it if you have it). Crack the eggs in the pan, and pour in the milk. Stir it up and then heat it up while still stirring. When the eggs start to solidify, toss in the veggies. When it is all solid, throw in the cheese and let it melt on top. Stir minimally during this part. Turn the heat off and scoop it into the tortilla. Add salsa to taste.

OMELETS OR SCRAMBLED EGGS WITH STUFF IN THEM

Eggs	3 if you are hungry, 2 if you're not, or if you're short on eggs
Milk	about 1/4 cup or less

Butter or no-stick spray stuff

Optional things to put in: (If you don't use any of these, you've just made scrambled eggs.)

Cheese	shred or cut into little bits, a piece about 1/2"–3/4" thick, more if you like them really cheesy
Green pepper	about 1/4 of the pepper (make sure to get the seeds out.)
Onion	Chop up enough to fit in the palm of your hand in a little pile
Mushrooms	as many sliced up as you want
Ham	Cut into little pieces as many as you want—usually about as much as the cheese.

Anything else you think would taste good… leftover bacon, garlic, and so on

Pots and pans to clean up—1 frying pan, 1 mixing bowl

Crack the eggs in the bowl. Add the milk. Stir it up with a fork. Set it aside while you cut up any of the stuff you want to add. Now, for the hard part. If you want to make an omelet, butter or spray the pan well. Carefully pour the eggs in and cook them slowly. Pull the edges of the omelet up as they solidify with a flipper and let the liquid run under. When the eggs are half-way cooked, add the fillings on top of the flat, cooked eggs. Keep pulling the edges up until it is all solidified then flip half of the cooked egg circle up over the other half, so that it's folded in half with the stuff inside.

If you just want scrambled eggs with stuff in them, skip the part about carefully pulling the edges back and just mix it all up until it is solid.

FAST-FOOD BREAKFAST SANDWICH

Eggs	1 or 2
Milk	a dash
Cheese	1 or 2 slices
Ham	1 slice of deli type ham (optional)
Bread	English Muffin, wheat bread, bagel, or whatever bread product you have in the apartment

Pots and pans to clean up—1 frying pan

Butter the pan or do something so it doesn't stick (spray that no-stick spray on it if you have it). Crack the eggs in the pan and pour in a dash of milk. Stir it up, then heat it up while still stirring until you've made scrambled eggs. Now you have a couple of options depending on your kitchen appliances:

If you have a toaster oven, put the eggs on the bread product, lay the ham and cheese on the eggs and pop it in the toaster oven until the bread is toasted and the cheese starts to melt.

If you have no toaster oven, toast the bread product, lay the ham and cheese on the eggs and leave it until the cheese melts. Then put the eggs, ham and cheese on the bread and you have your own version of the fast food classic breakfast sandwich.

PANCAKES ❧

Eggs	1
Milk	1 cup
Oil	2 tablespoons
Flour	1 cup
Sugar	1 tablespoon

Baking powder	2 teaspoons
Salt	between 1/2 and 1/4 teaspoon
Baking soda	1/2 teaspoon

Pots and pans to clean up—1 bowl, 1 frying pan

If you want my opinion, buy *Bisquick* or something like that and follow the recipe on the box. This is doable, but those mixes make perfectly good pancakes. So, if you are into a lot of work in the morning, or are trying to impress that somebody special, go for this recipe. It makes about 6 to 8 pancakes.

Crack the egg in the bowl and beat it with a fork. Add the milk and oil. Stir it up. Then add the flour, then the other stuff and stir it all up. Butter or spray a frying pan, heat it up and pour the mix out into as many cakes as will fit in your pan. Flip them with a flipper thingamajig until they are as done as you like them. That's all.

WAFFLES ❧

Waffle iron	Without this you just aren't going to make these.
Waffle mix	You know, it comes in a box…

Pots and pans to clean up—waffle iron, 1 bowl

Just save me the trouble of writing out ingredients for this one and go buy a mix. Follow the instructions on the box. The complete mixes aren't as good as the ones where you need to add an egg or something like that. Spray no-stick stuff on the waffle maker irons (easy), or butter it when it is hot (a real pain). Turn it on, dump the batter into the waffle maker. Close it, and wait for the light to go off. I highly recommend one with a light, otherwise you get some really interesting, but inedible, results.

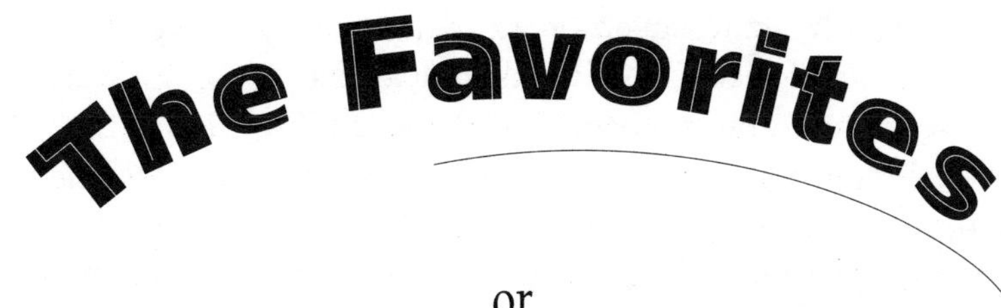

The Favorites

or

Things I Make Pretty Often

I guess the title of this one is self explanatory. I like these, I make them a lot, and usually they come out okay. I also didn't know where else I could put these, so I made this category.

FRIED RICE WITH CHICKEN (OR BEEF OR SHRIMP)

Chicken	1 chicken breast, boneless, about 1/4 pound
Rice	instant rice, 1 cup
Green pepper	about 1/3 of the pepper, chopped up
Onion	same amount as the pepper, chopped up
Garlic	1 clove
Carrot	1 peeled and sliced into little pieces
Water chestnuts	5 or 6 sliced up
Egg	1
Soy sauce	as much as you want
Pepper	a dash or two
Oil	a dash for the bottom of the pan

Pots and pans to clean up—1 sauce pan, 1 frying pan

If you're using a frozen chicken breast, defrost it, but leave it a bit cold. The microwave works well for this. So does putting it in a pan of hot water. Make the instant rice, according to the package directions. While that is going, chop up all the vegetables and cut the chicken into thin slices. Add the oil to the frying pan, and heat it up. (If you have a wok, use it instead.) Add the chicken, and stir it around until it turns white all the way through. While it is cooking, dash soy sauce in the pan. (like 3 or 4 shakes of the bottle.) Check to see if the chicken is done by cutting a piece in half. If it is still pink, keep cooking it. When it is done, push it to the side and crack the egg in the pan. Break the yolk, and mix it around until it is scrambled. Then pour in all of the vegetables and a dash or two of pepper. Add more of the soy sauce, and keep mixing it for about 2 minutes. Then add the rice to the pan. Add more soy sauce to the rice and mix it all up for about another 3 to 5 minutes. That's all it takes.

All of the things I put in were found by experiment or seeing them in fried rice in Chinese restaurants. I suggest you mess with the measurements and ingredients until you have your own recipe. My opinion is that the water chestnuts are optional, and if you have them, great, otherwise, no big deal. I just treat beef or shrimp like the chicken, and it works.

STIR FRY DINNERS (CHICKEN, BEEF, SHRIMP, PORK, AND SO ON)

Chicken	1 chicken breast, boneless, about 1/4 pound
Rice	instant rice, 1 cup
Green pepper	about 1/3 of the pepper, chopped up
Onion	same amount as the pepper, chopped up
Garlic	1 clove, chopped up
Carrot	1 peeled and sliced into little pieces
Water chestnuts	5 or 6, sliced up

Broccoli	about 1 handful, or 2 frozen stalks, chopped up
Snow Peas	10 or 12 pea pods
Soy sauce	as much as you want
Pepper	a dash or five (depends on taste)
Oil	a dash for the bottom of the pan
Cornstarch	optional, or flour (This is if you want a sauce.)

Pots and pans to clean up—1 sauce pan, 1 frying pan

If you are thinking this looks remarkably like the fried rice recipe above, you're right. Except for leaving out the egg and adding broccoli and pea pods, it is. Make the chicken the way you made the fried rice, but don't pour in the broccoli and snow peas with the other veggies. When you get to the part about adding the rice, don't. Instead, add 1/2 cup of water and about 1 teaspoon of cornstarch. Stir this around, add some more soy sauce and you will get some kind of sauce. Then add the broccoli and pea pods. The key on these is not to cook them too long, otherwise they get really mushy. So cook them while the sauce continues to thicken (about 2 minutes). Place the whole stir fry mixture on top of the white rice.

CHICKEN WITH HAM AND CHEESE

Chicken breast	1 boneless piece
Deli ham	1 slice
Cheese (your choice)	1 slice large enough to cover the chicken

Pots and pans to clean up—1 baking tray

This one is basically foolproof. Defrost the chicken, lay the slice of ham on it and place it on a tray in the oven at 400° for about 25 minutes. If the tray isn't no-stick, grease the tray with butter or no-stick spray first. You may want to do this anyway–it makes it taste a little better. If your roommates lost a bet and have to do your dishes, then maybe don't grease the pan. Check the chicken to see that it is white all the way through. If it is, lay the slice of cheese on the chicken and ham and put it back in the oven for about 3 minutes. This dish goes well with rice.

TACOS

Ground beef	1/2 pound or so
Green pepper	about 1/4 of a pepper cut into small pieces
Onion	same amount as pepper, also in small pieces
Salsa	as much as you want
Taco seasoning	use half of a ready-made packet, or about 2 teaspoons each of chili powder and cumin, or just some salsa if that's all you've got
Tortillas	as many as you want (Taco shells are okay too.)
Cheese	shred a pile about as big as a handful
Lettuce	same as cheese
Tomato	about 1/4 of a tomato, cut into little pieces
Black olives	optional (Slice a pile as big as the tomato pile.)

Pots and pans to clean up—1 frying pan

Brown the ground beef in the frying pan. Add the green pepper and onion while it's cooking. Drain the grease and add the taco seasoning. Let that cook for 5 minutes, while cutting up all of the other things. I recommend microwaving the tortillas for about 10 seconds each, just because I like them hot. Fill the totillas or taco shells with meat and add all the other stuff you cut up.

FAJITAS, EITHER BEEF OR CHICKEN ❧

Chicken or steak	1/4–1/3 pound chicken breast or any kind of cheap steak
Green pepper	1/2 a pepper, sliced length wise, no seeds

Onion	1/2 of an onion, sliced so you have long strips
Cheese	Shred a pile about as big as a handful.
Lettuce	same as cheese
Tomato	about 1/4 of a tomato, cut into little pieces
Tortillas	as many as you want (Taco shells are OK too.)
Salsa/Picante sauce	enough to cover the meat
Tabasco sauce	optional (A dash or two.)
Black olives	optional (Slice a pile as big as the tomato pile.)

Pots and pans to clean up—1 frying pan, 1 bowl

Defrost the meat but leave it slightly frozen so it is easy to cut. Slice it into thin strips. Poke a fork into the strips so there are some holes through it for the sauce to soak in. Put it in a bowl and pour some picante sauce over it to marinate it. You can add a dash of tabasco sauce if you want. Let it soak for about 20 minutes, longer if you have the time. While it is soaking, cut up the other vegetables. When it is done soaking, take the meat out and put it in a hot frying pan. Add the onions and green peppers when the meat is about half-way cooked (so they stay crunchy). Keep the meat moving around so it cooks evenly and pour some of the marinade over the meat while it's cooking. Check to see if it is done by cutting a piece open. If you are making chicken, make sure it is all white throughout. Remove it from the heat, than go ahead and pile up a tortilla with meat and vegetables and cheese.

CHICKEN AND FETTUCCINI ❦

Chicken breast	1 boneless (about 1/4 pound)
Fettuccini noodles	a handful
Spaghetti sauce	about a cup
Garlic	1 clove, chopped up
Oil	dash, for the pan

Pots and pans to clean up—1 frying pan, 1 sauce pan

First, heat the water for the fettuccini in the sauce pan until it boils. When the water is boiling, add the fettuccini. Let it boil for about 10 minutes.

Slice the chicken breast up into strips. Pour a dash of oil in the frying pan and add the chicken and garlic. If you want, you can add butter instead of oil—some people think it tastes better. Fry (or "sauté" if you want someone to think you are a chef) the chicken until it is white all the way through. Lower the heat and let it sit for a bit.

Strain the fettuccini, then pour the spaghetti sauce into the pan it was in. Dump the fettuccini back into the pan with the sauce and heat it on low heat for about 5 minutes, or until it is hot all the way through. Stir it every few minutes. Then add the chicken to the mix. Or, you can put the fettuccini on your plate and place the chicken on top of it. This looks good, and will make your roommates (or date) envious of your cooking abilities.

TERIYAKI STEAK OR CHICKEN

Steak	1 steak, about 1/3 lb
or	
Chicken	1 boneless breast
Teriyaki sauce	1/4 of a bottle (depends on size) or 1 package

Pots and pans to clean up—1 broiler pan, 1 bowl to soak the stuff in

This one is easy, but takes awhile. First, defrost the chicken or steak about half way, so it is still kinda stiff. Cut it into thin slices and poke each slice with a fork several times. Mix up the package of teriyaki sauce if you've got a package. Toss the meat into a bowl, and pour the sauce over it. Some people recommend using a zip-loc bag, and that way you can mix it up easily. I usually don't have any bags, so I use a bowl. Put the bowl/bag in the fridge for about 1 hour. If the sauce doesn't cover the meat completely, turn it over after 1/2 an hour so all the meat gets to soak in the sauce.

Now, lay the strips down on a broiler pan and pour about half of the remaining sauce on the strips. Put the pan in the oven on broil, about 4 inches away from the heat source. After about 8 minutes, pull it out, turn the meat and pour the sauce over the other side. Let it cook for another 5 minutes or so. These times are really just guesses, since different broilers work differently. Keep checking them every few minutes, so you don't get burned chicken or steak.

This meal works well with white rice. Makes you feel like you had more than just a bunch of meat for dinner.

PIZZA (EASY VERSION)

Phone	1, touch tone or rotary dial
Money	hopefully, no more than 7 bucks; maybe up to $10

Pots and pans to clean up—0, none, nada, zip, zilch, get the point?

Call _ _ _-_ _ _ _ (fill in your favorite or cheapest pizza place in town). Wait 30–45 minutes. If you really want to cook your own pizza, look in the Meals to Impress Your Date section of this book.

STUFFED BAKED POTATOES

Potato	1 large baking potato
Ground beef	optional (about 1/4 pound)
Green pepper	A little bit, maybe 1/6 of a pepper, diced
Onion	1 very small one, or half of a large one chopped up
Carrot	1, peeled and sliced into small bits
Cheese	slices or grated to cover potato
Broccoli	one small handful, chopped up finely
Bacon	optional, but three or four slices of bacon can replace the beef

Pots and pans to clean up—1 frying pan, one baking tray or microwave dish

First, wash the potato, then poke it with a fork several times. Either bake the potato in an oven or toaster oven (50 to 60 minutes at 425° F) or nuke it in a microwave (6 or 7 minutes depending on your microwave—turn it half way through). While that is going on, brown the beef or cook the bacon if you want the version with meat. If you are using beef, toss the onion and green pepper in the frying pan to cook with the beef. You might want to leave them out altogether if you are using bacon.

When the potato is done, cut it in half and scoop out part of it. Mash the scooped out part with a fork and put it back in the potato with the meat and the vegetables. Microwave it for about 1 minute (or oven for 5 minutes). Add the cheese to the top and either nuke or bake it until the cheese melts. That's all for this meal.

Healthy version, lower fat and all that: Skip the beef, light on the cheese.

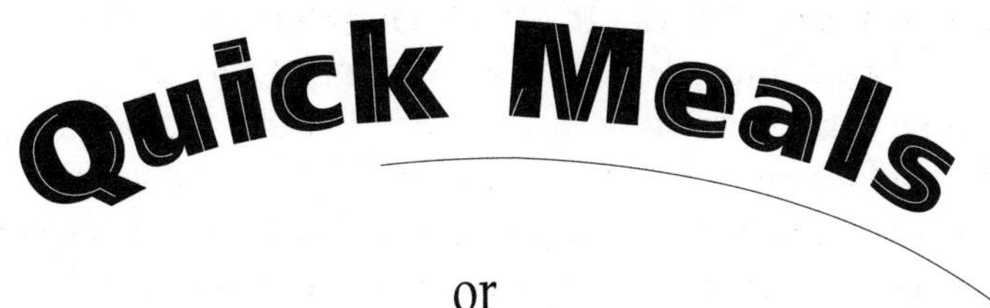

Quick Meals

or

I gotta go to (insert your own activity here) at 7 and I am really hungry and I only have 45 minutes to eat.

Here is a section which I have to consult a lot during the actual school year. It's necessary when you have 2 tests to study for, a paper due, and a meeting all in the same night. The key to these isn't great taste, price or ease of clean up. This is a section about speed. We're talking 15 to 20 minutes, tops. Most are quicker.

SPAGHETTI

Spaghetti noodles	about 1" inch diameter bunch—about as many as fit in the O in an OK sign
Spaghetti sauce	I cover the bottom of a saucepan, usually. I also recommend *Prego*. And no, I didn't get paid for that.
Ground beef	optional, about 1/4 of a pound or less

Pots and pans to clean up—1 saucepan, 1 strainer, 1 frying pan (optional)

The tried-and-true favorite. The big thing here is having a jar of spaghetti sauce. If you don't, look for the recipe later that says how to make your sauce when you have time. It is under "pizza" in the Meals to Impress Your Date section. But this one here is fast, and for that, you need a jar of sauce.

Fill a saucepan about 1/2–3/4 full with hot water (takes less time to boil). Put a lid on it (once again, quicker and it saves energy), and put it on the stove. Boil it. While waiting for it to boil, if you want to brown the hamburger in a frying pan, go ahead. When the water boils, toss in spaghetti. Lower the heat a bit so it doesn't boil over, but make sure the water is still bubbling so the spaghetti moves around. Let it cook for about 9 minutes. Take it out, pour it in the strainer and let it sit in there during the next step.

Pour the sauce in the already hot sauce pan, heat it and stir it up for about 2 minutes, then dump spaghetti in again. You can dump the hamburger in now too. Bingo, dinner time.

GRILLED CHEESE AND GRILLED HAM AND CHEESE

Sliced bread	any kind, 2 slices per sandwich
Cheese	either American, 1 slice per sandwich, or slice your own favorite cheese into enough thin slices to cover a piece of bread
Butter	enough to butter however many slices you have
Ham	optional, 1 slice per sandwich

Pots and pans to clean up—1 frying pan

Butter one side of the bread. Heat up the frying pan, then put a bit of butter in the pan so the stuff doesn't stick. Lay a slice of bread butter side down in the pan, then a slice of cheese on the bread. The ham goes on now if you want. Butter another slice of bread while that is cooking. Check the bread by lifting the corner with a flipper or spatula. When it is the color you want, put the other slice of bread on the sandwich butter side up, then flip it over. Check it until you like the color. Repeat this for more sandwiches.

SLOPPY JOES—A WARPED VERSION

Hamburger	1/3 pound or so
Barbecue sauce	enough to cover the hamburger
Onion	chopped up, a small pile in your palm
Green pepper	same as onion
Hamburger buns or bread	

Pots and pans to clean up—1 saucepan

Brown the hamburger in the saucepan with the onion and green pepper. When it is all cooked, drain the grease. Pour in barbecue sauce and simmer for about 3 to 5 minutes while stirring. Put on the buns or bread and your sandwiches are done.

Some people use that canned Sloppy Joe mix, but I don't like it. Mine's probably an acquired taste. Like a fungus, it grows on you.

SOUPS

1 can of soup	your favorite type
5 or 6 crackers	optional

Pots and pans to clean up—1 saucepan, 1 can opener

Did you expect a "how to make your own soup" in the quick meals section? This is just a discussion on which canned soups are okay. Overall, they make a good quick meal that is cheap and easy to make but during the summer they never taste that good and of course, every once in a while, it is nice to chew a meal.

CAMPBELLS—Well, they are cheap, pretty good and you probably had these when you were a kid because they have been around forever. I like cream of chicken,

chicken noodle and tomato. A can makes 1 to 2 servings if you follow the instructions on the can. The part about stirring in the liquid slowly for the cream of chicken is really true. If you add the liquid all at once it comes out kind of chunky.

CHUNKY—Not bad, but more expensive than the traditional Campbells. You can add a bit of water to each can to stretch it, but a small can will never be more than one serving.

PROGRESSO—Once again, not bad. It doesn't have the big hunks of meat and potatoes that Chunky does, but it tastes pretty good.

HOME COOKIN'—My favorite. You can add a bit of water to the can, but once again a small can is only one serving. I like Tomato Garden with crackers, Country Vegetable, and Chicken with Noodles.

POWDERED SOUPS—I don't like 'em. I might eat them if somebody gave them to me for free; maybe, if I was really hungry—but I doubt it. But if you put them in sour cream or yogurt, they make great chip dips (my wife has done this).

MACARONI AND CHEESE WITH STUFF IN IT

Macaroni and cheese	1 box
Milk	whatever amount the box suggests
Butter	as above
Canned chicken	optional, as much as you want
Hot dogs	optional, as much as you want
Broccoli	same
Salsa	same
Anything else you have leftovers of	

Pots and pans to clean up—1 saucepan

Well, there isn't much you can't do with macaroni and cheese. Personally, I get sick of it after a while and rarely eat it anymore. But it is nice to have a box on reserve just in case you are really hungry and rushed for time.

Make the mac and cheese by the box instructions. Toss in whatever you want. I've tried all of the above, but don't limit yourself. Be creative. Stir it around with the heat on, then get the additions warm. Hey, it isn't gourmet dining but you can live on it if you have to.

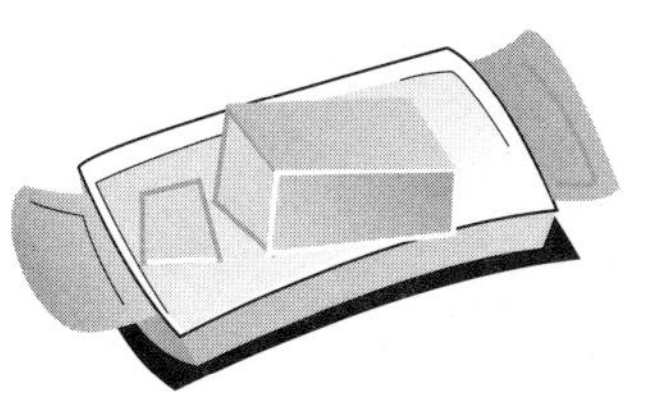

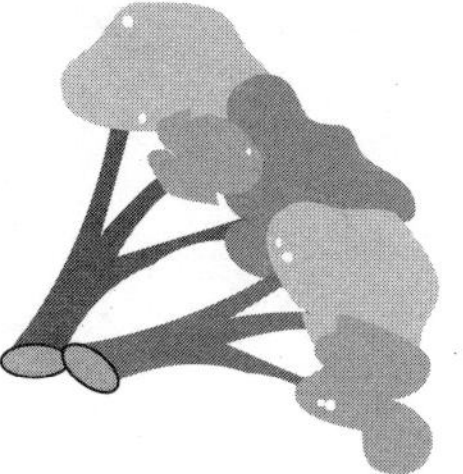

BEANS AND FRANKS

Pork and beans	1 can
Hot dog	1 or 2

Pots and pans to clean up—1 saucepan, 1 can opener

Well, this doesn't take a rocket scientist. There isn't much to it. But then, none of the recipes in this section have much to them. That was the whole point.

Heat the pork and beans in a saucepan. Stir it around so it doesn't burn on the bottom of the pan. Cut up the hot dogs and toss them in the pan. Keep stirring until the hot dogs get warm. That's all there is to it.

Things That are hard to make for one meal or one person

or

Leftovers Aren't All That Bad.

Every once in a while, I come across a great recipe that just can't be cooked for 1 serving. These meals are great if you don't mind eating leftovers for the next couple of days. Some times the problem is that one ingredient only comes in a certain size and you need to use it all up or it goes bad. Some of those are here because it takes absolutely no more work to make 3 servings than one serving, so you may as well get as much food for your effort as possible. These are dishes you will either want to save for leftovers or make for those rare occasions when you want to cook for your roommates.

CHICKEN AND WILD RICE ❧

Chicken — 1 boneless breast
Wild rice — 1 box of Uncle Ben's Wild Rice (instant is nice)
Oil, butter or spray stuff, enough so your chicken doesn't stick
Green pepper — optional
Onion — optional
Lemon — optional

Pots and pans to clean up—1 frying pan, 1 sauce pan

First, defrost the chicken. While that is going on, make the wild rice according to the package directions. (They can vary by brand, so I'm not giving you any.

Go ahead, read the box.) While the rice is cooking, cut up the chicken and sauté (cool word, huh? Just means add a bit of butter or oil and stir the chicken around until it is white all the way through) the chicken until it is done. You can also add green pepper, onion, garlic, or lemon juice if you want.

The rice should be finished about now, so drain any excess oil from the chicken and then dump it in the rice. Stir it up and you're set.

This makes enough for two meals.

CHILI

Ground beef	1/2–2/3 of a pound
Green bell pepper	1/2 or 3/4 of a whole bell pepper, chopped up
Onion	1 small (smaller than a baseball), chopped up
Garlic	2 cloves chopped into very small pieces
Red kidney beans	16 ounce can
Can of tomatoes	16 ounce can or so
Tomato paste	6 ounce can
Salt	a couple dashes
Pepper	more than the salt
Chili powder	2 teaspoons, or more if you like it spicy
or	
Tabasco sauce	2 or 3 dashes

Crackers and shredded cheese to put on top are optional

Pots and pans to clean up—1 large sauce pan

Cut up the onion, green pepper and garlic. Put them in the saucepan with the ground beef and cook until the beef is brown. Drain out any grease but not the vegetables. Open the tomatoes and cut them up inside the can by slicing around with a knife. Pour the whole can, including liquid, in the saucepan. Drain the kidney beans and add them too. Add the tomato paste then fill the tomato paste can 3/4 full of water and add that to the mixture. Add the salt, pepper and spice. Stir it all up, put a lid on the pan so it doesn't splatter all over the kitchen, and keep it on low to medium heat for 15 minutes or so. Makes 3 meals, maybe 4.

SAUTÉED CHICKEN GARDEN SALAD ❧

Chicken breast	1/4 pound boneless
Lettuce	1/3–1/2 a head of lettuce, shredded
Carrot	1 large carrot, peeled and sliced
Tomato	1, cut into about 8 slices
Green bell pepper	1/4–1/2 of a pepper
Onion	1/2 of a small one
Garlic	1 clove, chopped up
Butter or margarine	about 1 tablespoon
Cheese	shredded, about 1 handful

1 hard-boiled egg, sliced up (optional)

Pots and pans to clean up—1 frying pan, 1 large bowl

Cut up all of the vegetables and set aside about 1/2 of the green pepper, 1/2 the onion and all of the garlic. Put these in the frying pan with the butter. Put all of the other veggies in a large mixing bowl. Slice the chicken breast up into thin strips.

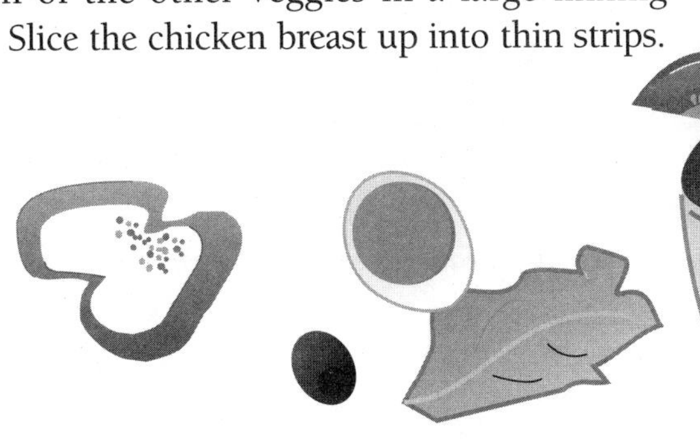

Turn on the range and heat up the butter and veggies until the butter melts. Add the chicken. Stir it around until the chicken starts to get brown marks. Cut open a piece to see if it is white all the way through. If it is, take the chicken out of the pan with a fork and add it to the salad. Don't pour the onions and green peppers you cooked with the chicken in the salad–they were just there to flavor the chicken. Also, remember you just sautéed something, so now you sound like a fancy chef, the kind of cook that knows when to sift flour. Serves 2 people, or you twice. Good in the summer.

PASTA SALAD ❦

Rotini	1 box of multicolored rotini (looks cool)
Black olives	1 can, sliced or whole (slice them yourself)
Tomatoes	2, sliced into 8 pieces each
Green pepper	1/2 of the pepper
Carrot	1, peeled and sliced up
Cucumber	about 3 or 4 inches of a cucumber, sliced up
Pepperoni	about 2 inches, sliced up or you could buy it already sliced in a little bag
Italian salad dressing	from a bottle, unless you have some secret family recipe

Any other veggies you like in whatever amounts you like

Pots and pans to clean up—1 large bowl, 1 large pan, 1 strainer

Boil water in the big pan. Add the rotini for about 10 minutes. While it is boiling, cut up all of the other stuff. When the rotini is done, drain it in the strainer, and rinse it in cold water. Put it and all of the other stuff in the large bowl and pour salad dressing on it until you like the way it tastes. Serves a lot. I usually bring this to picnics my department has, if they want you to bring food. It is easy to make and it is a lot cooler than bringing another bag of chips.

Side Dishes

or

What to do when you want more stuff on your plate (including vegetables).

Well, in the odd case that you do not want to just have one thing to eat and you have a burning desire to have a (do I dare say it?) second course, then you may want to peruse this section. Sometimes, just chicken and ham and cheese is just not enough–you want to fill up on something else. Plus, for those of you who feel that the selections in the next chapter (Meals to Impress Your Date) may look better with something else on the plate, you would turn here for the inspiration to create that balance on the plate that will amaze and astound that someone special. I bet there are people out there who would take that last sentence seriously. I bet they aren't reading this…

FRUIT SALAD ❧

Pineapple	1 can of sliced or chunk pineapple
Bananas	1 or 2, sliced into disks
Strawberries	1/2 pint or more if they're in season (sliced up)
Peaches	2, sliced up
Kiwi	1, with skin peeled off and then sliced up

Pots and pans to clean up—1 bowl

I make this a lot when I grill, because a couple of bratwurst doesn't make a whole meal. To assemble your fruit salad, open the can of pineapple, pour it in a bowl (if you want, you can drain some of the juice but I like having it there–it makes everything taste a little different) and add the other stuff you have. This usually makes about 4 servings. Of course, the ingredients should be determined by what you have around and what you like. The only recommendation I have is to stay away from oranges. I love them, but everyone else picks them out when I include them. So, I guess citrus fruit in this might not fly for most of you, but hey, try it if you want.

BAKED POTATO OR TWICE BAKED POTATO

Potato	1 large baking potato
Sour cream	1/4 cup
Salt	a dash
Pepper	another dash
Cheese	optional, 1 slice or a bit grated

Pots and pans to clean up—1 baking sheet or microwave dish, 1 bowl

Wash the potato and prick it with a fork several times. Either bake the potato in an oven or toaster oven (50 to 60 minutes at 425°) or nuke it in a microwave (6 or 7 minutes, depending on your microwave; turn it half way through). If you are making a baked potato, you are done now.

If you are making a twice baked, then take the potato out and cut off part of the top so you can spoon some of the insides out. Scoop out the potato, leaving just a little around the skin. Put the insides in a bowl and add the sour cream, salt and pepper. Beat it with a masher or mash it with a fork until it is pretty smooth.

Put the mixture back in the potato (it will pile over the top a little) and put the cheese on top if you have it. Put it into an oven for 15–20 minutes at 425°.

SCALLOPED POTATOES

Potatoes	1 really large or 2 medium, sliced thinly
Onions	about half an onion, chopped up
Butter	1 teaspoon
Flour	1 teaspoon
Milk	1/2 cup
American cheese	1/2 cup, shredded
Salt and pepper	to taste (wing it; not much of either)

Pots and pans to clean up—1 casserole dish (I know, but you need it), 1 sauce pan

Put the butter or margarine in the sauce pan, toss in the onion and heat it up until you have a sauce. Stir in the flour, the milk and a dash of salt and pepper. Mix it up, then add the cheese and stir until it is melted and bubbling. Grease the casserole dish and put in about 1/2 the potatoes. Pour about 1/2 the sauce over them, then add the rest of potatoes and sauce. Bake at 350° (covered if possible) for 30 minutes, then uncover and bake for another 30 minutes.

Healthy version—less fat and cholesterol and all that stuff : Skip the cheese.

RICE PILAF ❧

Rice	1 cup instant rice
Carrots	1, shredded or chopped up really fine
Onion	1/2 of one, chopped up
Green pepper	optional, a small handful chopped up is nice
Pepper	about 5 shakes with my shaker
Garlic	optional, maybe 1 clove chopped up really fine

Pots and pans to clean up—1 sauce pan

Well, pour 1 cup of water into a sauce pan. Add all of the vegetables and then heat it until boiling. Toss in the rice, stir it around, remove from the heat, cover it and let it stand until the water is all soaked up. Stir it around and you're in business. This goes really well with just about anything.

FROZEN VEGETABLES AND ADDITIONS ❧

Frozen vegetables	Whatever type you want
Other stuff	See below

Pots and pans to clean up—1, usually

Well, what we have here is a list of other stuff you can add to frozen vegetables to spice them up a bit and make them a little less bland. Of course, feel free to experiment.

BROCCOLI:	Onions, red peppers, green onions, lemon juice, cheese, carrots
GREEN BEANS:	Onions, bacon, cheese, carrots
CORN:	Tomato, onion, dash of pepper
CAULIFLOWER:	Cheese

PEAS:	Carrots, onions
BEETS:	About 1/4 cup vinegar with a can of beets (chill them)
SPINACH:	A little vinegar

BROCCOLI AND CARROT STIR FRY

Broccoli	1/2 bag of frozen broccoli or fresh broccoli cut up
Carrots	3 or 4 sliced up
Garlic	1 clove, chopped up
Soy sauce	several dashes
Lemon juice	optional, but a few dashes works well
Oil	just a dash on the bottom of the pan

Pots and pans to clean up—1 fry pan (or wok)

Put the oil in the pan, heat it up and toss everything in. Stir around for about 3 or 4 minutes. Don't go too long or the broccoli gets really chewy. It's better if it is still crisp.

Meals to Impress Your Date

or

Looks good, tastes good and not too hard to make.

Okay, so sometimes you want to look good for somebody and you invite him or her over for dinner. Usually, it's a lot cheaper than going out and it can be a lot more fun. You don't have to deal with some goof ball waiter who gets the orders wrong, or a 45-minute wait because they don't take reservations, or getting stuck at a table next to the amazingly loud family with the four year old who really isn't having a good time. All of that goes away if you cook dinner yourself. The only problem you have now is your roommates. I know they can act like the above mentioned four year old, but there's a chance they're going out to eat, so you could have the place to yourself. Anyway, these recipes are a little harder to make and may involve a trip to the grocery store the day before, but it could be worth it... after all, one of these may turn out to be good. These recipes are for two, in case you didn't get the point of the chapter title.

SWORDFISH (OR SHARK) KABOBS

Fish	1/2 a pound of swordfish or shark steaks
Green pepper	about 3/4 of a pepper, cut into 1" squares
Onion	1, sliced up into about 1" squares
Mushrooms	real ones, not canned, about 6, each sliced into quarters
Cherry tomatoes	about 4, sliced into quarters
Garlic	1 clove, cut up into tiny pieces

Oil	about 1/4 cup
Wine	white, about a 1/4 to 1/2 cup
Peels	optional, teaspoon of shredded orange, lime, or lemon peel
Plastic bag that zips closed	
Rice	

Pots and pans to clean up—1 bowl, 1 broiler pan, 4 or 8 shish kabob skewers (depending on whether they are the short one or long ones)

Get started on this one kind of early. Cut up the fish steaks into 1" cubes. Cut up the garlic but try not to hold onto it—it makes your hands stink and that really puts a damper on a date. Just chop it up with a knife. Grate the peels if you want. Mix the oil, wine, garlic and peels in a bowl. If you want, squeeze in some juice from the fruit. Put this mixture into a plastic bag (or a covered tupperware container) and dump in the fish. Let it sit for about 30–45 minutes.

Cut up the other veggies during this time. 1" squares are nice. Slice the tomatoes so they still look like circles. Then, pull the fish out of the bag and stick everything on skewers, alternating the foods. Place them on a broiler pan and spoon about half of the sauce on them. Broil them about 4 or 5 inches from the heating element for 5 minutes. Take them out, turn them over and spoon on the rest of the sauce. Go another 5 or 6 minutes.

Serve this on a bed of rice. Either make white rice, like instant rice, or wild rice. They both go well.

RIBS

Baby back ribs	1 or 2 slabs, depending on size of slab
Onion	1 medium onion
Tabasco	2 or 3 dashes of Tabasco sauce
Garlic	2 cloves
Vinegar	about 1/8 cup
Barbecue sauce	1 cup
Worcestershire sauce	1 tablespoon

Pots and pans to clean up—1 large baking pan, 1 grill

Okay, obviously you need a grill for this one. Also, you're going to need charcoal to make the grill work. Plus, if your date doesn't dig getting messy while eating, ribs are probably a lousy choice. But hey, I think this is a pretty impressive dinner. My girlfriend (now wife) dug it.

First, grate the onion. This is going to make you cry, but deal with it, it is worth it. Cut up the garlic into small bits. Pour about 1 cup of barbecue sauce, 1 tablespoon of Worcestershire sauce and the vinegar into a baking pan. Add the garlic, onion and a dash or two of Tabasco. Stir it all up and lay the ribs on the mixture, meaty side down. Scoop up some of the sauce on the ribs. Cover this mix and let it sit for about 3 hours (some people go up to 12 or 24, but I never have that much patience) in the fridge.

Start up the grill about 1 hour before you want to start grilling. Let the charcoal turn gray before you start.

Put the ribs on the grill about 4 or 5 inches from the coals. After 15 minutes, turn the ribs and baste them with sauce. If the side that was cooking looks raw, lower the grill closer to the fire. If the ribs look charred, raise the grill. Turn after another 15 minutes. Then, continue turning and basting every 5 minutes for about another 30 minutes.

Be careful not to let the fire flame up and scorch the ribs. When you are done, take them off the grill and enjoy. You can serve them with baked potatoes or onion rings. And hey, if your date doesn't enjoy these, you just get more to eat. It's kind of cool because cooking them takes a long time and you can both hang out while grilling.

PIZZA (THE HARD, BUT REALLY COOL 'CAUSE IT'S FROM SCRATCH, WAY)

DOUGH RECIPE

Flour	2 1/4 cups white flour
Salt	1/2 teaspoon
Olive oil	2 tablespoons (tablespoons, the big ones!)
Yeast	1 package of dry yeast
Water	3/4 cup water
Brown sugar	1 teaspoon

Pots and pans to clean up for dough—1 bowl, 1 cutting board

This is going to make the dough, but it will take time. Plan ahead is my point. I like thick crust, so this is for thick crust. If you like thin crust, I'll tell you how to do that too.

Take 1/4 cup warm (not hot) water and stir in the brown sugar and the package of yeast. Hot water will kill the yeast (and your hopes of a pizza crust), so try to keep it about 115°. Set this aside for at least 5 minutes or until it foams up.

While the yeast is chugging away, dump 2 cups of flour into a big bowl and add the salt. Make a hole in the pile and dump in 1 and 1/2 tablespoons olive oil and 1/2 cup warm water. Then, when you have foamy yeast water, dump it in too.

Dust the cutting board (or whatever you choose to knead the dough on) with some flour (more than 2 cups). Mix up the mixture in the bowl with your hands until it kinda sticks together. Put it on the board, and knead it for about 5 or 10 minutes (it'll stick together into a ball-like thing) by rolling it over and pressing it down over and over and over…

Clean out your mixing bowl and wipe it dry. Then, wipe it down with olive oil. Also rub oil over the ball of dough. Put the dough in the bowl and cover it with a towel. Put it in the oven for 1 hour (the oven is dark and the dough will rise. **Do not turn on the oven yet!** This would be a good point to look ahead on how to make the sauce (since you have a bunch of time to kill).

If you want thin crust, let the dough rise for 1 and 1/2 hours total. But, if you are like me and want thicker crust, after 1 hour, pull the dough out and smash it down. Then cover it and put it back in the oven for about another 45 minutes.

Sauce

Olive oil	4 tablespoons
Garlic	2 cloves
Onion	2, chopped up into small bits
Canned tomatoes	2 28-ounce cans, drained
Basil	1 or 1 and 1/2 teaspoons
Tarragon	2 teaspoons
Oregano	3 teaspoons
Salt	2 teaspoons
Tomato paste	6-ounce can
Pepper	several dashes

Pots and pans to clean up—1 big sauce pan

This makes enough sauce for two pizzas. The point is that you can put it in the fridge for up to a couple of weeks or use it for pasta or anything else that would go good with a tomato sauce. If you are going to go through all of this work to make the sauce, you might as well make a bunch.

Pour the oil in the sauce pan. Heat it up (medium) and while it heats, chop up the garlic and onion. Add them to the oil and let them heat until the onions turn clear. While that is going on, take out the tomatoes and chop them up into tiny bits. Add them to the sauce pan. Then, dump in all of the spices and such. You look really cool if you measure the herbs into your hands and grind them up into the sauce, like the chef you are trying to be.

Let this simmer for about 45 minutes to an hour.

Now, move on to actually making the pizza.

ASSEMBLING THE PIZZA

Dough	see above
Sauce	3 cups of the sauce above
Mozzarella cheese	3 or 4 cups, shredded
Parmesan cheese	couple dashes out of the container
Olive oil	enough to brush over the crust and pan
Pepperoni	about 20 slices (3 or 4 inches of a sausage)
Green pepper	2 handfuls
Onion	1 handful
Mushrooms	2 handfuls
Anything else you like	

Pots and pans to clean up—1 pizza pan or 1, 9" x 12" baking dish, rolling pin

For thick crust pizza, warm the oven up to 350°. For thin crust, turn it to 500°. After the dough has risen, roll it out to about the shape of the pan. Since I don't own a pizza pan for deep dish pizza, I use a 9" x 12" baking pan. Hey, so my pizza is square, it still tastes good.

Oil the pan with the olive oil and lay the dough in it. If you want thick crust, oil the top of the dough and let it sit in the pan for 10 minutes. Then, pop it in the oven for about 15 minutes. Take it out and you will see that the dough has risen. If you are making thin crust, just oil the pan, put the dough in and oil the dough.

Now, assemble the pizza. Put the sauce on the crust, then the toppings and then the cheeses. For thick crust, toss it back in the oven (at 350°) for another 20 minutes. For thin crust, put it into the oven at 500° for 10 or 15 minutes. For both of these, check on the pizza. If the cheese is completely melted (but not crusting) you are done.

Bingo, you just made a pizza. Sure it was time consuming and tiring and took a lot of stuff you usually don't use, but it might be worth it. Plus, you probably have enough left over for lunch tomorrow.

QUICHE—LEFTOVER FLAVOR

Eggs	3
Milk	1 and 1/2 cups
Onions	1/2 of a small onion, or 3 green onions, chopped up
Green pepper	about 1/4 of a pepper, chopped up. Don't use too much
Salt	a couple of shakes
Pepper	a couple of shakes
Cheese	1 and 1/2 cups of shredded cheese (about 1 big handful)
Meat	ham, turkey, bacon, or my personal favorite, hamburger or chicken or any other meat you have left over.

Flour	1 tablespoon
Parsley	optional, but a little bit can't hurt
Mushrooms	same as parsley, use them if you have them

Ready-made pie crust—not the graham cracker one, but one that is refrigerated

Pots and pans to clean up—1 pie pan, 1 bowl

This one is kind of cool and I've started to use it a lot to get rid of leftover vegetables and meat. See, I baked a ham the other day because it was really cheap and I thought that it would be kind of a cool meal to impress that someone special. Unfortunately, that left me with a boatload of extra ham and I had to come up with something to do with it. Luckily my wife (yep, this book has taken a while to finish) suggested I try this. I think it worked.

Chop up all of the vegetables and shred the cheese. Then, put the pie crust in the pie pan (instructions should be on the back of the box) and put it in the oven at 325° for 10 minutes. While that is going on, break the 3 eggs in a bowl, add the milk and mix it up really good. Then, add the vegetables. Dump the flour on the cheese and then put that in the bowl and mix it up really well.

Take out the pie shell and pour the mixture into it. Put it back into the oven for about 35–45 minutes. Start checking it to see if it is done by putting a knife in the center. If it comes out with egg stuff on it, put it back in the oven and wait some more. I have found the time on this depends on how many vegetables you put in. Too many green peppers seemed to make it take longer.

Anyway, I think that's about it for this one. I usually have enough leftover for one or two more meals.

Cookies and Fun Foods

or

Hey, these taste good!

After cooking for a while, you realize that sometimes you just want things that taste good. These are commonly called desserts. With a few basic ingredients, you can crank out stuff cheaper and better than you can get at a supermarket. Plus, the status of being able to cook good desserts is unequaled. You may impress people with your ribs, or a pizza, or a good stir fry, but you'll knock them dead with junk food! I guess, in a way they belong in the Meals to Impress Your Date section of the cookbook, since they do have that effect. But, then you wouldn't look there if you just wanted dessert for yourself. And, I think they deserve their own section. Plus, you are less likely to chow all of these at once, because you want to savor them since you put the time and effort into cooking them. Or, at least that is what I say before I eat about 1/2 of a banana bread in a day. You know, a slice or three for breakfast, one for dessert at lunch and then another at dinner time. Pretty soon I'm out, but hey, that's why I made it—to eat, not to look at.

Some quick tips on baking. I have learned most of these the hard way.

1. There is a difference between baking powder and soda. Read the ingredients!
2. If a recipe calls for cream of tartar powder, even if it is only 1/4 teaspoon, it means it. Don't leave it out. Snickerdoodles turn out like rocks without it.
3. Grease the pan if it says so.
4. If brown sugar turns rock hard in your cabinet, you can microwave it and it softens enough that you can measure it. Be careful. Zap it too long and you'll have a smoking mass of brown lava.

5. Vanilla is in just about everything. Make sure you have a bottle. The imitation stuff works too. I have not been able to tell the difference.
6. An electric mixer is never needed, but can be a real bonus. Maybe your roommate has one…
7. The bottom of a broiler pan works as a cookie sheet. Most electric ovens come with one, unless your landlord is a real cheapskate.
8. The ingredients for these are less flexible than the ingredients for other recipes in this cookbook.

Unless you are pretty sure of the effects of substituting something (like coconut for nuts) I would recommend staying with what's here.

CHOCOLATE CHIP COOKIES

Flour	2 1/4 cups
Sugar	3/4 cup
Brown sugar	3/4 cup, packed
Vanilla	1 teaspoon
Baking soda	1 teaspoon
Salt	1 teaspoon
Butter	2 sticks (1 cup)
Eggs	2
Chocolate chips	1 12-ounce bag, semi sweet chocolate chips

Pots and pans to clean up—1 bowl, 1 or 2 cookie sheets

Take the butter or margarine out of the fridge and let it soften. You want it definitely soft for this. Put the soft butter, sugar, brown sugar and vanilla in a bowl. Mix it up until it is pretty creamy. Add the eggs and stir some more. Then, add the flour, baking soda and salt. Stir it all up and add the chips. Keep mixing until it is smooth and the chips are evenly mixed.

Heat the oven to 375°. Put spoonfuls of dough on the cookie sheet at least 2" apart. They should be smaller than golf balls. Bake them for 9 or 10 minutes. Let them cool a little before you take them off the cookie sheet.

You can also make these in a pan version. Just spread the dough over the bottom of a shallow baking pan. Bake at 375° for about 20 or 25 minutes.

CHOCOLATE CHIP—COCONUT BARS

Flour	1 1/2 cups
Brown sugar	1/2 cup
Butter or margarine	1 stick (1/2 cup) cold
Sweetened condensed milk	14 oz. can
Chocolate chips	12-ounce bag
Vanilla	1 teaspoon
Egg	1
Coconut (or nuts)	1 or 1 1/2 cup (depends if you like it)

Pots and pans to clean up—1 bowl, 1, 9"x12" baking pan

This one is kind of neat. I like it and not many other people make it. Pour the flour and brown sugar into a bowl. Cut the cold butter in and mix it up. It will get kind of crumbly. Then, add 1/2 of a cup of coconut and about 1/3 of the chips and mix that in. This is your crust. Press it into the bottom of the pan and bake it at 350° for 15 minutes.

While it is cooking, pour sweetened condensed milk, the egg and vanilla together. Mix it up, then add the remaining coconut. Kind of depends on how much you like it. If you think it shouldn't be there, you can use walnuts or something else. Add the remaining chocolate chips.

Spread this mixture over the crust and bake for 20 or 25 minutes. Pull it out and let it cool before cutting into bars. Store them at room temperature, not in the fridge.

SNICKERDOODLES

Flour	1 1/2 cups
Sugar	1 cup
Butter	1 stick (1/2 cup)
Egg	1
Vanilla	1/2 teaspoon
Baking soda	1/4 teaspoon
Cream of tartar	1/4 teaspoon
Cinnamon	1 teaspoon

Pots and pans to clean up—1 bowl, 1 or 2 cookie sheets

Beat the butter in a mixing bowl until it looks sort of creamy. Helps if you let the butter soften a little. Add half of the flour, the sugar, egg, vanilla, cream of tartar and soda. Mix it all up until it is uniform, then add the rest of the flour and continue mixing. Finally it should be all mixed up.

Cover the bowl and put it in the fridge for 1 hour. Heat the oven to 375°. Take the cinnamon and maybe 3 tablespoons or so of sugar and mix them up in another small bowl. Form the cookies into 1" balls and roll them in the sugar and cinnamon mixture. Put them on the ungreased cookie sheet and pop them in the oven for about 9 or 10 minutes. Let them cool a little before taking them off the sheet.

CHEESECAKE

Cream cheese	2 8-ounce packages
Sugar	1/2 cup
Vanilla	3/4 teaspoon
Eggs	2
Graham cracker crust	1 9" round, ready-made crust

Pots and pans to clean up—1 bowl

Mix the cream cheese, sugar and vanilla until smooth. An electric mixer really helps on this. Otherwise, you are in for some serious work. Add the eggs and mix some more. Pour this into the pre-made crust and bake at 350° for 40 minutes or so. Cool, then refrigerate to store it.

BANANA BREAD

Flour	1 3/4 cups
Sugar	2/3 cup
Baking powder	2 teaspoons
Baking soda	1/2 teaspoon
Salt	dash or two
Bananas	2 that have gone brown
Butter	1/3 cup (that's about 2/3 of a stick)
Milk	2 tablespoons
Eggs	2

Pots and pans to clean up—1 bowl, one loaf pan

Peel the bananas and mash them up in a bowl. Let the butter soften a bit and add it and the milk. Pour in 1 cup of the flour, the sugar, baking power, baking soda and the salt. Mix until this is blended up really well. Then, add the rest of the flour and the eggs and mix it up again.

Grease a loaf pan (you really need one of these for this recipe) and put it in the oven at 350° for 55 minutes. Check the center of the loaf with a sharp knife. If it comes out gooey, put it in again until it comes out clean. Don't go over 1 hour 5 minutes, though. Let it cool for about 15 or 20 minutes and then knock it out of the pan. Wrap it in aluminum foil and store at room temperature.

PLAIN FROSTED COOKIES

COOKIE PART OF RECIPE

Sugar	1 cup
Butter	1 cup
Egg yolks	3
Flour	2 1/4 cup
Salt	1/2 teaspoon

TOPPING INGREDIENTS

Egg whites	1 tablespoon
Vanilla	1 tablespoon
Sugar	1/2 cup

Pots and pans to clean up—1 mixing bowl, 1 small bowl, 1 or 2 cookie sheets

Mix together sugar and butter for cookies until it is creamy. Mix in egg yolks, flour and salt. Mix stuff for topping in a small bowl. Drop cookies in little round balls on cookie sheet, flatten them a little, then dent the top and put a little topping in. Bake at 350° for 6–8 minutes.

CHOCOLATE CAKE—BROWNIE WITH CHOCOLATE CHIP TOPPING

Flour	1 3/4 cup
Sugar	1 cup
Baking soda	1 teaspoon
Boiling water	1 cup
Cocoa	1 tablespoon
Salt	1/2 teaspoon
Egg	1
Oil	1/2 cup

Vanilla	1 teaspoon
Nuts	1/2 cup, chopped up (if you like nuts)
Brown sugar	1/2 cup
Chocolate chips	1 cup

Pots and pans to clean up—1 bowl, 1, 9"x9" baking pan.

Put boiling water in measuring cup and add the baking soda. A glass measuring cup, one with a handle, would be a good choice unless you like burning yourself. In the mixing bowl, stir together flour, sugar, cocoa, salt, egg, oil and vanilla. Add the nuts if you want. Stir it up well, then pour it into a greased 9x9 (or some similar size) baking pan. Once it is in the pan, sprinkle the brown sugar on top of it. After the brown sugar is sprinkled, drop the chocolate chips on top of it. "Why the order for this?" you ask. The answer is, I do not know and haven't actually tried it the other way around. I know it works this way and comes out tasting really good. So, either experiment and take a chance, or go with the flow on this one.

Anyways, after you have sprinkled the stuff on top of the cake mixture, put it in the oven at 350° for 30 minutes. Let it cool before you cut it and after you cut it you can store it in the fridge to keep the topping chewy.

GINGERBREAD

Flour	1 and 1/2 cups
Egg	1
Brown sugar	1/4 cup packed down
Cinnamon	3/4 teaspoon
Ginger	3/4 teaspoon
Baking powder	1/2 teaspoon
Baking soda	1/2 teaspoon
Margarine	1/2 cup
Molasses	1/2 cup
Water	1/2 cup

Pots and pans to clean up—1 8" x 8" baking dish, 1 bowl

Put all of the dry things into a bowl and stir them around. Grease the baking dish with the paper from the margarine and then put a little flour on the dish and shake it around to cover the bottom. Add everything that isn't in the bowl already to the bowl and beat for either a really long time by hand or with an electric mixer for a couple of minutes. Pour the mixture into the dish and bake it at 350° for about 35 minutes. Check the center by poking a knife into it. If it comes out dry, it is done. Make sure to let it cool down a bit before cutting it up, because otherwise you kind of tear it up.

Wrap Up

or

The part that is just for reading and ideas, with no real recipes.

Well, this has been an interesting undertaking for me. When I started on this, I was just finishing up my undergraduate degree. That's a BS in Materials Science Engineering for those of you interested, so you know I was just doing this for fun and not taking classes or anything special for this. I'm finishing this right as I start my Ph.D. In the time it has taken me to do this, I got my Masters. So, this truly is a college student's cookbook. I promise that I really was a college student throughout the entire writing of this book.

I've also had varied testers on these recipes, about 6 different roommates, their girlfriends, and my wife (yes, the intro said girlfriend, it really has been a long time writing this). So, I should thank them all again and for all of the friends at Purdue who kept saying, "Hey, that's a cool idea."

But, enough about me. How about some things about this whole cooking concept. As I have seen many people eat peanut butter and jelly over and over and over, I hope this book can keep you from this trap. That's the whole idea of cooking food like this for yourself. You get to eat pretty well-rounded and relatively healthy meals for not much money and usually not much time investment.

Of course, my cooking styles have changed over the course of the last two years. I've tried to cut down on the fat and cholesterol and I hope that shows up in some of the recipes. I've marked the ones that could be considered healthy with a ❦. Okay, this is a joke, I just did it to hopefully make points with your parents so they think this is a really cool gift and they get one for you and your cousin. It can't hurt.

Plus, on a slightly higher plane of thought, going to college was supposed to help you grow and learn things and become a well rounded asset to civilization. So in a way, this could be thought of as a textbook for a non-credit class. Hopefully they won't sell this one used at the bookstore, because the author never sees any of that money. Of course, I'll try to make sure they don't charge $65.00 for this, like most of my textbooks. Wow, think of this excuse: If you're like me, when you get really busy with homework you always come up with something else that needs to be done. So, now you can cook dinner and say to yourself that you're really doing homework.

Speaking of that, what if I actually had written this as a textbook? Could you imagine the homework assignments I could have come up with? Chapter 1, problem 4 for Wednesday. I don't care if you have a test that day, you still have to make the Chicken Stir Fry. Yes, I only allow 21 people in the class and each of you are going to be responsible for 1 meal a week. Then, I could eat for free for the next semester. As long as nobody tries to argue with the grading, I think I could get away with it. Maybe I'd give all A's unless I got sick from something you made. It is enough to make me rethink my career choice.

Anyway, I think I've babbled enough. I really hope you have enjoyed this and that it got you away from the frozen dinners and chicken patties every night. I really have enjoyed cooking all of these and hope you do to. I could finish with some very wise saying, but I'm afraid that that would be way too predictable. So instead, I'll leave you with an idea from my masters thesis. Molybdenum alloyed in stainless steel will lessen pitting corrosion in environments containing halides by changing the passive film. Who knows, that may prove more helpful than the recipes. But I doubt it.

Ciao (pun intended).

Index

-T-

-W-

ABOUT THE AUTHOR

Dave Bahr has been a college student since the fall of 1988 and will continue at the University of Minnesota until his PhD in Materials Engineering is finished. It may take a while. Originally from a suburb of Chicago, he went to Purdue, in West Lafayette, Indiana for his BS and MS in Materials Engineering. By the way, if anyone knows what a Hoosier is, let him know. He can now be reached in Minneapolis, where he and his wife live in an apartment with a cat which acts a lot more like a dog than a cat and another that acts like a rock. He's been cooking since moving into an apartment his junior year and has managed not to fall into the trap of peanut butter and jelly sandwiches and repeated macaroni and cheese dinners for over 3 years. This is his first attempt at writing a cookbook, or any type of book for that matter.

All COOL HAND titles are available through your local bookstore or by mail. To order directly, return the coupon below to: COOL HAND COMMUNICATIONS, INC., Order Department, 1098 N.W. Boca Raton Blvd., Boca Raton, FL 33432.

Title	ISBN	Price	Quantity
New for 1994 (COOL HAND Creations)			
MEN: The Handbook	1-56790-113-1	$11.95	______
Bobby Joe: In The Mind of a Monster	1-56790-093-3	$12.95	______
The College Student's Cookbook	1-56790-059-3	$5.95	______
The Myth of Medicine	1-56790-027-5	$11.95	______
The Ultimate Italian Pastries	1-56790-103-4	$9.95	______
Recently Released			
How to Cope With Chronic Pain	1-56790-043-7	$9.95	______
National Park Vacations: The West-Vol. 1	1-56790-012-7	$9.95	______
Creative Costumes for Children	1-56790-059-3	$11.95	______
Life & Love in the Paradise Lounge	1-56790-115-8	$6.95	______
Unfinished Business	1-56790-000-3	$22.95	______
Lynn Allison Better Lifestyle Series:			
1001 Ways/Life Better	1-56790-097-6	$7.95	______
The Magic of Garlic	1-56790-098-4	$7.95	______
Natural Stress-Busters	1-56790-099-2	$7.95	______
Uncommon Footsteps	1-56790-149-2	$19.95	______
Hit of the Party	1-56790-063-1	$19.95	______
World's Worst Cookbook	1-56790-137-9	$8.95	______
Cool Hand Classics			
Think A Little	1-56790-025-9	$7.95	______
Compleat Option Player	0-89709-200-7	$14.95	______
Creative Costumes	1-56790-056-9	$6.95	______
Dr. Cookie's Cookbook (Comb)	1-56790-109-3	$7.95	______
Dr. Cookie's Cookbook (Paper)	1-56790-108-5	$6.95	______
Early American Cookbook	1-56790-087-9	$7.95	______
Muffin Mania	1-56790-074-7	$7.95	______
One Day Celestial Navigation	1-56790-021-6	$12.95	______
		Sub-total	______
		Please add $2.00 for postage and handling.	______
		Florida residents add 6.5% sales tax to order.	______
		TOTAL	______

Bill To:

____

____

____

Ship To: ______________________________

____

____

____